MW00896644

Applying Fractions
Grade 4

Table of Contents

Free Video Tutorial

 Use this QR code to launch a short video that provides instruction for skills featured in this book. To access the video from your smartphone or tablet:

- Download a free QR code scanner from your device's app store.
- Launch the scanning app on your device.
- Scan the code to visit the web page for this book.
- Find the video under the Resources tab.

This *Spectrum Focus* video is also available at:
- http://www.carsondellosa.com/704904
- www.youtube.com/user/CarsonDellosaPub

Spectrum®
An imprint of Carson-Dellosa Publishing LLC
P.O. Box 35665
Greensboro, NC 27425

© 2016 Carson-Dellosa Publishing LLC. Except as permitted under the United States Copyright Act, no part of this publication may be reproduced, stored, or distributed in any form or by any means (mechanically, electronically, recording, etc.) without the prior written consent of Carson-Dellosa Publishing LLC. Spectrum® is an imprint of Carson-Dellosa Publishing LLC.

Printed in the USA • All rights reserved.   ISBN 978-1-4838-2421-5

01-204157784

Focus On Applying Fractions

Proficiency in working with fractions is a critical building block in students' journey toward mathematical understanding. Creating equivalent fractions is essential for comparing fractions. Adding and subtracting fractions with like denominators can be used to solve a variety of real-world problems. Multiplying fractions by whole numbers is another strategy for solving word problems. Finally, knowledge about fractions can be extended to decimal numbers. For each of these topics, *Applying Fractions* provides step-by-step teaching, explanations, and practice.

Equivalent Fractions

Equivalent fractions describe equal parts of the same-size whole. Look at the example. In both rectangles, the same fraction of the whole is shaded. One has 5 parts, and the other has 10. Four out of 5 parts is the same size as 8 out of 10 parts. So, $\frac{4}{5}$ and $\frac{8}{10}$ are equivalent fractions.

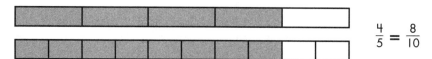

$$\frac{4}{5} = \frac{8}{10}$$

Look at another example. The first rectangle has twice as many parts as the second and twice as many shaded parts as the second. You can divide the numerator and denominator of $\frac{10}{12}$ by 2 to find the equivalent fraction $\frac{5}{6}$. You can multiply the numerator and denominator of $\frac{5}{6}$ by 2 to find the equivalent fraction $\frac{10}{12}$. An easy way to find an equivalent fraction for any fraction is to multiply or divide its numerator and denominator by the same number. This is the same as multiplying or dividing the fraction by 1 because $\frac{2}{2} = 1$, $\frac{4}{4} = 1$, etc.

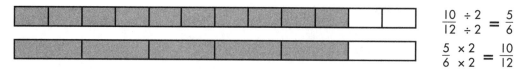

$$\frac{10 \div 2}{12 \div 2} = \frac{5}{6}$$

$$\frac{5 \times 2}{6 \times 2} = \frac{10}{12}$$

Creating Common Denominators

When two fractions have the same denominators, we say they have *common denominators*. Fractions with common denominators are easier to compare.

You can change any pair of fractions into fractions with common denominators. Look at the two original denominators and think of the *lowest common multiple*

Focus On Applying Fractions

they share. For example, the lowest common multiple of both 3 and 4 is 12. Create equivalent fractions that use this common multiple as a denominator. One simple way to create fractions with common denominators is to multiply the numerator and denominator of each fraction by the denominator of the other. Look at the examples below. The new fraction pairs $\frac{5}{15}$ and $\frac{6}{15}$ and $\frac{18}{24}$ and $\frac{20}{24}$ have common denominators.

Comparing Fractions

There are several ways to compare fractions that are different parts of the same-size whole. One way is to find a common denominator for the two fractions and then compare the numerators to see which is greater. To compare $\frac{1}{2}$ and $\frac{3}{4}$, create equivalent fractions that have a common denominator. Then, compare the numerators. Because 4 is less than 6, $\frac{4}{8}$ is less than $\frac{6}{8}$, and $\frac{1}{2}$ is less than $\frac{3}{4}$.

$$\frac{1 \times 4}{2 \times 4} = \frac{4}{8} \enspace \textcircled{<} \enspace \frac{6}{8} = \frac{3 \times 2}{4 \times 2}$$

Another way to compare fractions is to think about each fraction in comparison to a benchmark fraction that you know well, like $\frac{1}{2}$. To compare $\frac{1}{3}$ and $\frac{4}{5}$, think about the size of each in comparison to $\frac{1}{2}$. The model below illustrates that because $\frac{1}{3}$ is less than $\frac{1}{2}$, and $\frac{1}{2}$ is less than $\frac{4}{5}$, $\frac{1}{3}$ must be less than $\frac{4}{5}$.

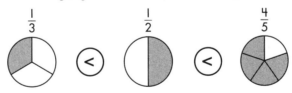

Adding and Subtracting Fractions with Like Denominators

When addends have a common denominator, find the sum of the numerators. The denominator stays the same. Look at different ways to find the sum $\frac{6}{8}$.

Focus On Applying Fractions

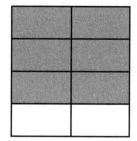

$$\frac{1}{8} + \frac{1}{8} + \frac{1}{8} + \frac{1}{8} + \frac{1}{8} + \frac{1}{8} = \frac{6}{8}$$

$$\frac{1}{8} + \frac{1}{8} + \frac{1}{8} + \frac{1}{8} + \frac{2}{8} = \frac{6}{8}$$

$$\frac{1}{8} + \frac{2}{8} + \frac{3}{8} = \frac{6}{8}$$

$$\frac{3}{8} + \frac{3}{8} = \frac{6}{8}$$

When the minuend and subtrahend have a common denominator, find the difference of the numerators. The denominator stays the same. Look at different ways to find the difference $\frac{1}{6}$.

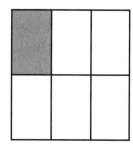

$$\frac{6}{6} - \frac{1}{6} - \frac{1}{6} - \frac{1}{6} - \frac{1}{6} - \frac{1}{6} = \frac{1}{6}$$

$$\frac{6}{6} - \frac{2}{6} - \frac{1}{6} - \frac{1}{6} - \frac{1}{6} = \frac{1}{6}$$

$$\frac{6}{6} - \frac{3}{6} - \frac{2}{6} = \frac{1}{6}$$

$$\frac{6}{6} - \frac{5}{6} = \frac{1}{6}$$

When you solve equations with fractions, always give the solution in *simplest form*. If possible, divide the numerator and denominator of your answer by the same number. This will create an equivalent fraction in simplest form.

$$\frac{8}{12} - \frac{2}{12} = \frac{6}{12} \begin{array}{c} \div 6 \\ \div 6 \end{array} = \frac{1}{2}$$

Adding and Subtracting Mixed Numbers

An *improper fraction* is a fraction whose numerator is greater than its denominator. The fraction $\frac{13}{3}$ is an improper fraction. You can change an improper fraction to the mixed number $4\frac{1}{3}$. *Mixed numbers* are combinations of whole numbers and fractions. Look at the example below.

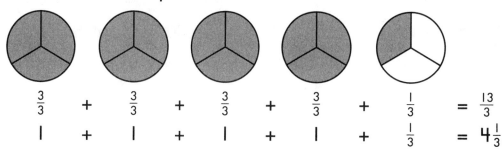

$$\frac{3}{3} \quad + \quad \frac{3}{3} \quad + \quad \frac{3}{3} \quad + \quad \frac{3}{3} \quad + \quad \frac{1}{3} \quad = \quad \frac{13}{3}$$

$$1 \quad + \quad 1 \quad + \quad 1 \quad + \quad 1 \quad + \quad \frac{1}{3} \quad = \quad 4\frac{1}{3}$$

Focus On Applying Fractions

To add and subtract mixed numbers, first add or subtract the whole numbers. Then, add or subtract the fractions.

$$3\tfrac{1}{4} + 7\tfrac{2}{4} = 10\tfrac{3}{4} \qquad\qquad 5\tfrac{5}{8} - 1\tfrac{2}{8} = 4\tfrac{3}{8}$$

To solve some problems, you may need to change mixed numbers to improper fractions. To do this quickly, multiply the denominator by the whole number and add the numerator. Write the answer over the denominator to create the improper fraction. See the example below.

$$
\begin{array}{r}
4\tfrac{1}{3} \\
- 1\tfrac{2}{3} \\
\hline
2\tfrac{2}{3}
\end{array}
\quad = \quad
\begin{array}{r}
\tfrac{13}{3} \\
- \tfrac{5}{3} \\
\hline
\tfrac{8}{3}
\end{array}
\quad
\begin{array}{l}
(3 \times 4 + 1 = 13) \\
(3 \times 1 + 2 = 5)
\end{array}
$$

Fractions as Multiples

The fraction $\tfrac{4}{5}$ represents 4 parts of a whole divided into 5 parts. You can show this by adding a unit fraction ($\tfrac{1}{5} + \tfrac{1}{5} + \tfrac{1}{5} + \tfrac{1}{5}$) or by multiplying the unit fraction by a whole number. The fraction $\tfrac{4}{5}$ is the same as $\tfrac{1}{5} \times 4$ because $\tfrac{1}{5}$ is repeated four times.

$$\tfrac{1}{5} \times 4 = \quad\quad\quad = \tfrac{4}{5}$$

Multiplying Fractions by Whole Numbers

You can multiply fractions by whole numbers in the same way. Imagine you have 3 boxes that are each $\tfrac{3}{4}$ full of soccer balls. How many whole boxes can be filled with soccer balls? To find out, you could add. But, multiplying makes it easier.

$$\tfrac{3}{4} \quad + \quad \tfrac{3}{4} \quad + \quad \tfrac{3}{4}$$

$$\tfrac{1}{4} + \tfrac{1}{4} + \tfrac{1}{4} \quad + \quad \tfrac{1}{4} + \tfrac{1}{4} + \tfrac{1}{4} \quad + \quad \tfrac{1}{4} + \tfrac{1}{4} + \tfrac{1}{4}$$

Focus On Applying Fractions

$$3 \times \frac{3}{4} = 9 \times \frac{1}{4}$$

$$\frac{3}{4} + \frac{3}{4} + \frac{3}{4} = \frac{1}{4} + \frac{1}{4} + \frac{1}{4} + \frac{1}{4} + \frac{1}{4} + \frac{1}{4} + \frac{1}{4} + \frac{1}{4} + \frac{1}{4}$$

$$\frac{3 \times 3}{4} = \frac{9 \times 1}{4}$$

$$\frac{9}{4} = \frac{9}{4}$$

$$2\frac{1}{4} = 2\frac{1}{4}$$

So, $2\frac{1}{4}$ boxes can be filled with soccer balls.

Fractions with Denominators 10 and 100

The fractions $\frac{1}{10}$ and $\frac{1}{100}$ look similar, but if you draw a model of each, you can see just how different they are in value.

$\frac{1}{10}$
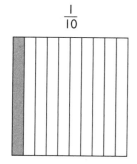

$\frac{1}{100}$
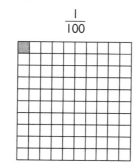

$\frac{1}{10}$ is ten times greater than $\frac{1}{100}$.

To change $\frac{1}{10}$ into the equivalent fraction $\frac{10}{100}$, multiply the numerator and denominator by 10.

$$\frac{1 \times 10}{10 \times 10} = \frac{10}{100}$$

Creating equivalent fractions that have the same denominator allows you to add them easily. To add $\frac{4}{10}$ and $\frac{19}{100}$, first change $\frac{4}{10}$ into an equivalent fraction with a denominator of 100. Multiply both the numerator and denominator by 10 to change tenths into hundredths. Then, add the numerators to find the sum.

$$\frac{4 \times 10}{10 \times 10} = \frac{40}{100} \qquad \frac{40}{100} + \frac{19}{100} = \frac{59}{100}$$

Look at the equivalent fractions below. Do you notice a pattern? A simple way to change tenths to hundredths is to add a zero to the denominator and numerator.

$$\frac{8}{10} = \frac{80}{100} \qquad \frac{6}{10} = \frac{60}{100} \qquad \frac{3}{10} = \frac{30}{100}$$

Changing Fractions to Decimals

The fraction $\frac{7}{10}$ is the same as the decimal 0.7. The fraction $\frac{76}{100}$ is the same as the decimal 0.76. You know that the first two place values to the right of the decimal point are tenths and hundredths. The fraction $\frac{76}{100}$ can be broken down into $\frac{7}{10} + \frac{6}{100}$ to show the tenths (7) and hundredths (6) digits.

Look at different ways to solve the addition problem below with fractions and decimals.

$$\frac{9}{10} + \frac{9}{100} = \frac{90}{100} + \frac{9}{100} = \frac{99}{100}$$

     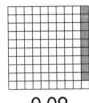

0.90   +   0.09   =   0.99

Comparing Decimals

You can compare decimal numbers that refer to the same whole. Use the following strategies to think about the comparisons below.

$$0.58 \textcircled{<} 0.73 \qquad 0.73 \textcircled{>} 0.58$$

Change Decimals to Fractions: You know that 0.58 is the same as $\frac{58}{100}$ and 0.73 is the same as $\frac{73}{100}$. Since the denominators are the same, the fraction with the larger numerator is greater.

Make a Place Value Chart: Make a chart to show the place value of each digit in the numbers. Then, compare the digits from left to right.

	Ones		Tenths	Hundredths
0.58	0	.	5	8
0.73	0	.	7	3

Make a Number Line: Find each number on a number line. The number 0.73 is closer to 1, so it is greater than 0.58.

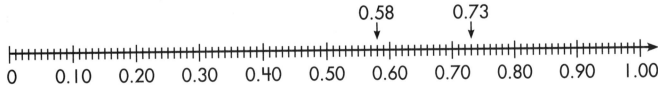

NAME _____

Guided Practice Equivalent Fractions

Follow the directions. Write a number in each box to answer the questions.

1. Look at the shaded part of the first shape. Color parts of the second shape to show an equivalent fraction.

2. Look at the shaded parts of the shapes. Write the equivalent fractions.

 =

3. Multiply the numerator and denominator by 3 to find an equivalent fraction.

$$\frac{1 \times 3}{6 \times 3} = \frac{\square}{\square}$$

4. Divide the numerator and denominator by 4 to find an equivalent fraction.

$$\frac{12 \div 4}{16 \div 4} = \frac{\square}{\square}$$

5. Write the factor used to create the equivalent fraction.

$$\frac{4 \times \square}{6 \times \square} = \frac{24}{36}$$

6. Write the divisor used to create the equivalent fraction.

$$\frac{30 \div \square}{35 \div \square} = \frac{6}{7}$$

7. Use multiplication to find an equivalent fraction.

$$\frac{4}{5} = \frac{16}{\square}$$

8. Use division to find an equivalent fraction.

$$\frac{10}{30} = \frac{\square}{3}$$

Independent Practice Equivalent Fractions

Write the equivalent fractions.

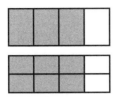

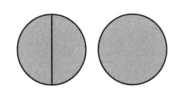

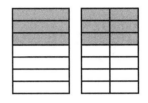

1. _____ = _____   **2.** _____ = _____   **3.** _____ = _____

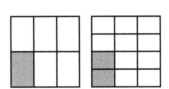

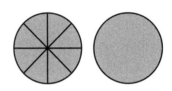

4. _____ = _____   **5.** _____ = _____   **6.** _____ = _____

To find an equivalent fraction, multiply the fraction by the number in the circle.

7. $\dfrac{5}{7} =$ ___ ⑨   **8.** $\dfrac{3}{6} =$ ___ ④   **9.** $\dfrac{2}{8} =$ ___ ④   **10.** $\dfrac{1}{6} =$ ___ ⑥

11. $\dfrac{1}{3} =$ ___ ⑨   **12.** $\dfrac{2}{3} =$ ___ ⑩   **13.** $\dfrac{2}{5} =$ ___ ⑤   **14.** $\dfrac{1}{8} =$ ___ ②

Complete the equivalent fractions.

15. $\dfrac{4}{5} = \dfrac{\Box}{10}$ **16.** $\dfrac{2}{\Box} = \dfrac{4}{6}$ **17.** $\dfrac{\Box}{8} = \dfrac{15}{24}$ **18.** $\dfrac{1}{4} = \dfrac{3}{\Box}$

19. $\dfrac{\Box}{20} = \dfrac{1}{2}$ **20.** $\dfrac{15}{\Box} = \dfrac{3}{5}$ **21.** $\dfrac{2}{8} = \dfrac{10}{\Box}$ **22.** $\dfrac{\Box}{12} = \dfrac{1}{3}$

Cross out the fraction that is not equivalent to the first.

23. $\dfrac{1}{5} =$ $\dfrac{2}{6}$ $\dfrac{2}{10}$ $\dfrac{3}{15}$ $\dfrac{4}{20}$ $\dfrac{5}{25}$ **24.** $\dfrac{2}{3} =$ $\dfrac{4}{6}$ $\dfrac{6}{9}$ $\dfrac{8}{16}$ $\dfrac{10}{15}$ $\dfrac{12}{18}$

Guided Practice Comparing Fractions

Follow the directions. Write a number in each box to answer the questions.

---

1. Circle the shape that has a greater shaded area.

2. Circle the shape that has less shaded area.

---

3. Write a fraction to name the shaded area of each shape. Then, write > (greater than), < (less than), or = (equal) in the circle to compare.

  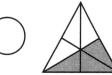

4. Write a fraction to name the shaded area of each shape. Then, write > (greater than), < (less than), or = (equal) in the circle to compare.

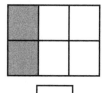 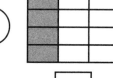

---

5. Complete the equivalent fractions. Then, write >, <, or = to compare.

$$\frac{3}{4} \bigcirc \frac{2}{3}$$

$$\frac{\Box}{12} \qquad \frac{\Box}{12}$$

6. Complete the equivalent fractions. Then, write >, <, or = to compare.

$$\frac{3}{6} \bigcirc \frac{5}{8}$$

$$\frac{12}{\Box} \qquad \frac{15}{\Box}$$

---

7. Compare.

$$\frac{2}{5} \bigcirc \frac{1}{4}$$

8. Compare.

$$\frac{1}{2} \bigcirc \frac{3}{5}$$

Independent Practice Comparing Fractions

Write each fraction. Then, compare using >, <, or =.

1.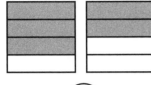

____ ◯ ____

2.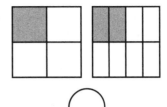

____ ◯ ____

3.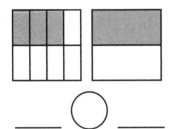

____ ◯ ____

4.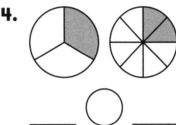

____ ◯ ____

Draw a picture for each fraction. Then, write >, <, or = to compare the fractions.

5. $\dfrac{7}{10}$ ◯ $\dfrac{3}{5}$

6. $\dfrac{3}{8}$ ◯ $\dfrac{3}{4}$

7. $\dfrac{1}{3}$ ◯ $\dfrac{5}{8}$

8. $\dfrac{1}{5}$ ◯ $\dfrac{2}{10}$

9. $\dfrac{3}{4}$ ◯ $\dfrac{1}{2}$

10. $\dfrac{6}{10}$ ◯ $\dfrac{2}{5}$

For each fraction pair, write equivalent fractions with a common denominator. Then, compare the fractions.

11. $\dfrac{4}{8}$ ◯ $\dfrac{2}{10}$

12. $\dfrac{1}{5}$ ◯ $\dfrac{2}{10}$

13. $\dfrac{3}{8}$ ◯ $\dfrac{10}{12}$

14. $\dfrac{3}{12}$ ◯ $\dfrac{1}{3}$

15. $\dfrac{2}{8}$ ◯ $\dfrac{1}{4}$

16. $\dfrac{3}{6}$ ◯ $\dfrac{4}{8}$

Guided Practice Adding and Subtracting Fractions

Follow the directions. Write a number in each box to answer the questions.

---

1. Color parts of the shape after the equal sign to solve the equation.

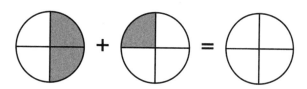

2. Color parts of the shape after the equal sign to solve the equation.

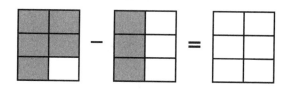

---

3. Write a fraction below each shape in the equation.

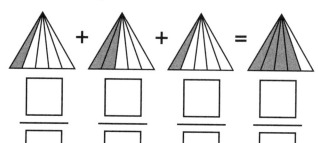

4. Write a fraction below each shape in the equation.

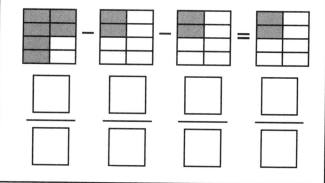

---

5. Complete the equation.

$$\frac{8}{15} + \frac{3}{15} = \frac{\square}{15}$$

6. Complete the equation.

$$\frac{8}{9} - \frac{4}{9} = \frac{\square}{9}$$

---

7. Complete the equation.

$$\frac{1}{8} + \frac{6}{8} = \frac{\square}{\square}$$

8. Complete the equation. Give your answer in simplest form.

$$\frac{10}{14} - \frac{4}{14} = \frac{\square}{\square} = \frac{\square}{\square}$$

Independent Practice Adding and Subtracting Fractions

For each fraction, write two equations. The first one should show the fraction as the sum of two or more fractions. The second one should show the fraction as a difference of two or more fractions.

1. $\dfrac{7}{8}$ **2.** $\dfrac{14}{16}$ **3.** $\dfrac{7}{10}$

_____   _____   _____

_____   _____   _____

Add or subtract. Give answers in simplest form.

4. $\dfrac{2}{4} + \dfrac{1}{4} =$ **5.** $\dfrac{6}{8} - \dfrac{4}{8} =$ **6.** $\dfrac{1}{5} + \dfrac{3}{5} =$

7. $\dfrac{7}{8} - \dfrac{5}{8} =$ **8.** $\dfrac{9}{10} - \dfrac{3}{10} =$ **9.** $\dfrac{6}{9} - \dfrac{2}{9} =$

10. $\dfrac{15}{20} - \dfrac{7}{20} =$ **11.** $\dfrac{68}{100} + \dfrac{12}{100} =$ **12.** $\dfrac{5}{50} + \dfrac{15}{50} =$

13. $\begin{array}{r} \dfrac{5}{12} \\[6pt] +\dfrac{3}{12} \\ \hline \end{array}$ **14.** $\begin{array}{r} \dfrac{3}{7} \\[6pt] +\dfrac{4}{7} \\ \hline \end{array}$ **15.** $\begin{array}{r} \dfrac{7}{10} \\[6pt] +\dfrac{2}{10} \\ \hline \end{array}$ **16.** $\begin{array}{r} \dfrac{3}{5} \\[6pt] +\dfrac{1}{5} \\ \hline \end{array}$

17. $\begin{array}{r} \dfrac{7}{11} \\[6pt] -\dfrac{5}{11} \\ \hline \end{array}$ **18.** $\begin{array}{r} \dfrac{8}{9} \\[6pt] -\dfrac{1}{9} \\ \hline \end{array}$ **19.** $\begin{array}{r} \dfrac{4}{5} \\[6pt] -\dfrac{2}{5} \\ \hline \end{array}$ **20.** $\begin{array}{r} \dfrac{8}{9} \\[6pt] -\dfrac{6}{9} \\ \hline \end{array}$

Guided Practice Mixed Numbers

Follow the directions. Write a number in each box to answer the questions.

1. Write a mixed number to represent the shapes.

 = $\boxed{}\dfrac{\boxed{}}{\boxed{}}$

2. Color the shapes to represent the mixed number.

$2\dfrac{2}{5}$ =

3. Write the improper fraction as a mixed number.

$\dfrac{16}{5}$ = $\boxed{}\dfrac{\boxed{}}{\boxed{}}$

4. Write the mixed number as an improper fraction.

$4\dfrac{1}{6}$ = $\dfrac{\boxed{}}{6}$

5. Add the whole numbers. Then, add the fractions.

$5\dfrac{2}{5} + 3\dfrac{1}{5}$ = $\boxed{}\dfrac{\boxed{}}{\boxed{}}$

6. Subtract the whole numbers. Then, subtract the fractions.

$8\dfrac{7}{9} - 6\dfrac{5}{9}$ = $\boxed{}\dfrac{\boxed{}}{\boxed{}}$

7. Change each mixed number into an improper fraction. Add. Change the sum into a mixed number.

$12\dfrac{3}{5}$ = $\dfrac{\boxed{}}{\boxed{}}$

$+\ 6\dfrac{4}{5}$ = $\dfrac{\boxed{}}{\boxed{}}$

$\dfrac{\boxed{}}{\boxed{}}$ = $\boxed{}\dfrac{\boxed{}}{\boxed{}}$

8. Change each mixed number into an improper fraction. Subtract. Change the difference into a mixed number.

$8\dfrac{5}{12}$ = $\dfrac{\boxed{}}{\boxed{}}$

$-\ 2\dfrac{10}{12}$ = $\dfrac{\boxed{}}{\boxed{}}$

$\dfrac{\boxed{}}{\boxed{}}$ = $\boxed{}\dfrac{\boxed{}}{\boxed{}}$

Independent Practice Mixed Numbers

Represent each group of shapes as a mixed number and as an improper fraction.

1. 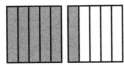 _____ or _____

2. 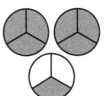 _____ or _____

3. 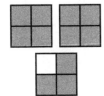 _____ or _____

4.  _____ or _____

Add or subtract. If needed, change the mixed numbers into improper fractions. Write each sum or difference as a mixed number in simplest form.

5. $9\frac{3}{10}$
$+2\frac{9}{10}$

6. $5\frac{1}{8}$
$+4\frac{3}{8}$

7. $1\frac{6}{7}$
$+3\frac{2}{7}$

8. $6\frac{4}{11}$
$+1\frac{3}{11}$

9. $3\frac{1}{10}$
$+4\frac{9}{10}$

10. $6\frac{5}{6}$
$+5\frac{5}{6}$

11. $7\frac{7}{9}$
$-4\frac{4}{9}$

12. $5\frac{7}{10}$
$-3\frac{1}{10}$

13. $6\frac{3}{5}$
$-4\frac{2}{5}$

14. $6\frac{4}{11}$
$-1\frac{3}{11}$

15. $4\frac{9}{10}$
$-3\frac{1}{10}$

16. $6\frac{5}{6}$
$-5\frac{5}{6}$

Guided Practice Multiplying Fractions

Follow the directions. Write a number in each box to answer the questions.

1. Write a fraction to show the sum.

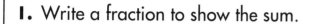 $= \dfrac{\Box}{\Box}$

2. Write a fraction to show the product.

 $\times 3 = \dfrac{\Box}{\Box}$

3. Write an improper fraction to show the sum.

$\triangle + \triangle + \triangle = \dfrac{\Box}{\Box}$

4. Write an improper fraction to show the product.

$3 \times \triangle = \dfrac{\Box}{\Box}$

5. Complete the product.

$$\dfrac{1}{10} \times 7 = \dfrac{1 \times 7}{10} = \dfrac{\Box}{10}$$

6. Complete the product.

$$5 \times \dfrac{3}{19} = \dfrac{5 \times 3}{19} = \dfrac{\Box}{19}$$

7. Write the product in simplest form.

$$\dfrac{1}{6} \times 4 = \dfrac{\Box}{\Box} = \dfrac{\Box}{\Box}$$

8. Write the product as a mixed number in simplest form.

$$8 \times \dfrac{4}{5} = \dfrac{\Box}{\Box} = \Box\dfrac{\Box}{\Box}$$

Independent Practice Multiplying Fractions

Multiply. Write answers in simplest form.

1. $5 \times \dfrac{2}{7} =$ _____

2. $3 \times \dfrac{4}{5} =$ _____

3. $7 \times \dfrac{6}{8} =$ _____

4. $2 \times \dfrac{3}{4} =$ _____

5. $4 \times \dfrac{2}{7} =$ _____

6. $6 \times \dfrac{1}{8} =$ _____

7. $8 \times \dfrac{1}{3} =$ _____

8. $2 \times \dfrac{3}{10} =$ _____

9. $\dfrac{8}{9} \times 3 =$ _____

10. $\dfrac{2}{5} \times 5 =$ _____

11. $4 \times \dfrac{3}{8} =$ _____

12. $6 \times \dfrac{1}{8} =$ _____

13. $3 \times \dfrac{5}{8} =$ _____

14. $4 \times \dfrac{1}{6} =$ _____

15. $\dfrac{1}{3} \times 9 =$ _____

16. $\dfrac{5}{9} \times 7 =$ _____

17. $\dfrac{7}{12} \times 2 =$ _____

18. $3 \times \dfrac{6}{7} =$ _____

19. $\dfrac{1}{2} \times 5 =$ _____

20. $6 \times \dfrac{2}{3} =$ _____

21. $\dfrac{1}{5} \times 4 =$ _____

22. $5 \times \dfrac{2}{3} =$ _____

23. $\dfrac{2}{7} \times 6 =$ _____

24. $3 \times \dfrac{2}{5} =$ _____

Guided Practice Solving Word Problems

Follow the directions. Write a number in each box to answer the questions.

1. In Shayla's horse figurine collection, $\frac{1}{8}$ are Arabians, $\frac{2}{8}$ are mustangs, and $\frac{3}{8}$ are ponies. Shayla arranged the Arabians, mustangs, and ponies on a shelf. How much of her collection was on the shelf?

$$\frac{1}{8} + \frac{\Box}{\Box} + \frac{\Box}{\Box} = \frac{\Box}{8} = \frac{3}{\Box} \text{ of the horse collection}$$

2. A trip to the amusement park will take $8\frac{4}{6}$ hours. The Johnson family has traveled for $2\frac{5}{6}$ hours. How much longer will it take the Johnsons to reach the park?

$$\frac{52}{6} - \frac{\Box}{\Box} = \frac{\Box}{6} = 5\frac{\Box}{\Box} \text{ hours}$$

3. Each day after school, Jonah read $\frac{1}{10}$ of his chapter book. He read for 5 days this week. How much of the book did Jonah read?

$$\frac{\Box}{10} \times 5 = \frac{\Box}{\Box} = \frac{\Box}{\Box} \text{ of the book}$$

4. For lunch on Thursday, 12 customers at a restaurant ordered soup. Each serving of soup was $\frac{2}{3}$ cup. How many cups of soup were served for lunch on Thursday?

$$\Box \times \frac{2}{3} = \frac{\Box}{3} = \Box \text{ cups of soup}$$

NAME _____

Independent Practice Solving Word Problems

Add, subtract, or multiply fractions to solve each word problem. Give answers in simplest form.

1. Jaleela has $4\frac{1}{8}$ gallons of blue paint and $2\frac{3}{8}$ gallons of gold paint. How much more blue paint does Jaleela have than gold paint?

Jaleela has _____ more gallons of blue paint.

2. In the cafeteria, $\frac{2}{7}$ of the students were fourth-graders and $\frac{3}{7}$ were fifth-graders. How many students were from the fourth and fifth grades?

_____ of the students were from the fourth and fifth grades.

3. It takes Carlos $2\frac{1}{6}$ days to make a model airplane and $1\frac{1}{6}$ days to make a model car. How many days will it take Carlos to make both?

It will take _____ days.

4. Autumn has a bag of apples. If she feeds $\frac{2}{4}$ of the bag to her favorite horse and $\frac{1}{4}$ to the new foal, how much of the bag is left?

_____ of a bag of apples is left.

5. Travis is $5\frac{7}{12}$ feet tall. Nathan is $6\frac{5}{12}$ feet tall. How much taller is Nathan?

Nathan is _____ foot taller than Travis.

6. One serving of pancakes calls for $\frac{1}{3}$ cup of milk. How many cups of milk are needed for 4 servings?

_____ cups of milk are needed.

7. If Carlos works $\frac{5}{12}$ of a day every day, how much will Carlos have worked after 5 days?

Carlos will have worked _____ days.

8. Each kite needs $\frac{2}{3}$ yard of string. How much string does Miranda need for 4 kites?

Miranda needs _____ yards of string.

Guided Practice Understanding Decimals

Follow the directions. Write a number in each box to answer the questions.

1. Circle an equivalent fraction and decimal number that show "three tenths."

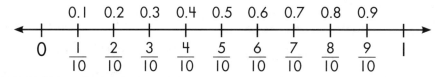

2. Circle an equivalent fraction and decimal number that show "sixty hundredths."

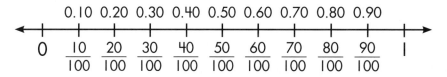

3. Write $\frac{9}{10}$ as a decimal number.

0.☐

4. Write $\frac{42}{100}$ as a decimal number.

0.☐☐

5. Complete the equivalent fraction so that both fractions have the common denominator 100.

$$\frac{6}{10} = \frac{\boxed{}}{100} \qquad \frac{21}{100}$$

6. Add.

$$\frac{60}{100} + \frac{21}{100} = \frac{\boxed{}}{\boxed{}}$$

7. Rewrite so that both addends have the common denominator 100. Add.

$$\frac{4}{10} + \frac{33}{100}$$

$$\frac{\boxed{}}{\boxed{}} + \frac{33}{100} = \frac{\boxed{}}{\boxed{}}$$

8. Rewrite so that both addends have the common denominator 100. Add.

$$\frac{2}{10} + \frac{63}{100}$$

$$\frac{\boxed{}}{\boxed{}} + \frac{\boxed{}}{\boxed{}} = \frac{\boxed{}}{\boxed{}}$$

NAME _____

Independent Practice Understanding Decimals

Find the number of tenths or hundredths in each model. Write the total as a fraction and as a decimal.

   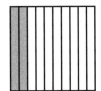

1. Fraction: _____   **2.** Fraction: _____   **3.** Fraction: _____

Decimal: _____   Decimal: _____   Decimal: _____

   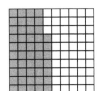

4. Fraction: _____   **5.** Fraction: _____   **6.** Fraction: _____

Decimal: _____   Decimal: _____   Decimal: _____

Rewrite fractions to create fraction pairs with common denominators. Then, add. Write answers in simplest form.

7. $\frac{1}{100} + \frac{9}{10} =$ **8.** $\frac{3}{10} + \frac{7}{100} =$ **9.** $\frac{9}{100} + \frac{9}{10} =$

10. $\frac{11}{10} + \frac{11}{100} =$ **11.** $\frac{2}{100} + \frac{3}{10} =$ **12.** $\frac{5}{10} + \frac{7}{100} =$

NAME _____

Guided Practice Comparing Decimals

Follow the directions. Write a number in each box to answer the questions.

1. Change each decimal number to a fraction. Circe the decimal number and fraction that are greater.

0.42 = ⬜/⬜   0.26 = ⬜/⬜

2. Write a decimal number for each model. Circle the decimal number that is less.

0.⬜   0.⬜

3. Find 0.54 and 0.45 on the number line. The greater number will be closer to 1. Circle it.

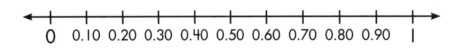

0   0.10 0.20 0.30 0.40 0.50 0.60 0.70 0.80 0.90   1

4. Write the decimal numbers eighty-five hundredths and fifty-eight hundredths in the place value chart. Draw a line through the number that is less.

Ones	Decimal Point	Tenths	Hundredths
0	.		
0	.		

5. Write > (greater than), < (less than), or = (equal to) to compare the numbers.

0.5 ◯ $\frac{1}{2}$

6. Write > (greater than), < (less than), or = (equal to) to compare the numbers.

0.20 ◯ 0.23

Guided Practice

Independent Practice Comparing Decimals

1. Locate $\frac{47}{100}$ and 0.83 on the number line. Circle the number that is greater.

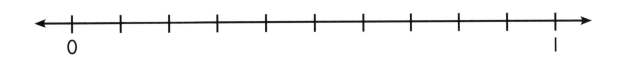

0   1

2. Locate $\frac{2}{10}$ and 0.8 on the number line. Circle the number that is less.

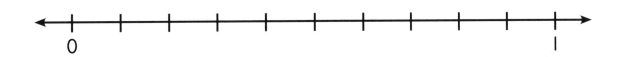

0   1

Write > or < to compare each pair of decimal numbers.

3. 0.6 $\bigcirc$ 0.4   **4.** 0.1 $\bigcirc$ 0.5   **5.** 0.23 $\bigcirc$ 0.03

6. 0.6 $\bigcirc$ 0.9   **7.** 0.06 $\bigcirc$ 0.60   **8.** 0.4 $\bigcirc$ 0.7

9. 0.9 $\bigcirc$ 0.5   **10.** 0.7 $\bigcirc$ 0.6   **11.** 0.42 $\bigcirc$ 0.14

12. 0.72 $\bigcirc$ 0.27   **13.** 0.25 $\bigcirc$ 0.52   **14.** 0.7 $\bigcirc$ 0.3

15. 1.4 $\bigcirc$ 1.6   **16.** 3.5 $\bigcirc$ 3.7   **17.** 16.2 $\bigcirc$ 16.8

Performance Task 1

Solve

Solve the real-world problem. Use the space to show your mathematical thinking.

Caleb says that $\frac{2}{4}$ is the same as $\frac{8}{16}$, but Marissa says it is the same as $\frac{1}{2}$. Who is correct? Why?

Reflect

In what real-life situation might it be useful to change $\frac{1}{2}$ of something into $\frac{2}{4}$ or $\frac{8}{16}$? Explain.

_____

_____

_____

_____

_____

_____

_____

Performance Task 2

Solve

Solve the real-world problem. Use the space to show your mathematical thinking.

Virginia has eaten 4 of the 6 slices of a pizza. Her mom tells her she has to give at least $\frac{1}{4}$ of the whole pizza to her brother. Does she have enough left to do that?

Reflect

Is there pizza left over? If so, what do you think is the fair thing for Virginia to do with it? Explain.

_____

_____

_____

_____

_____

_____

_____

Performance Task 3

Solve

Solve the real-world problem. Use the space to show your mathematical thinking.

A carpenter had a board that was $2\frac{5}{12}$ feet long. He cut off an 8-inch section. How long is the board now?

Reflect

Draw a picture of a yardstick to show your answer to the problem above.

Performance Task 4

Solve

Solve the real-world problem. Use the space to show your mathematical thinking.

In Hector's closet, $\frac{3}{5}$ of the clothing has stripes, $\frac{2}{3}$ of the clothing is blue, and $\frac{1}{4}$ of the clothing is pants. None of the pants have stripes. If 60 items of clothing are in Hector's closet, what is the greatest number of items that could be shirts without stripes?

Reflect

How could drawing a model help you solve the problem?

_____

_____

_____

_____

_____

_____

_____

Performance Task 5

Solve

Solve the real-world problem. Use the space to show your mathematical thinking.

Becky's teacher gave her the 7 tiles below. She was instructed to sort the tiles into three piles: closest to 0, closest to 0.5, and closest to 1. Sort the tiles for Becky and then create and sort additional tiles to have an equal number of tiles in each pile.

1.05	0.43	0.76	0.21	0.09	0.9	0.67

Reflect

What would be the greatest digit in the tenths place of the decimals in the "closest to 0" pile? Explain.

_____

_____

_____

_____

_____

_____

_____

NAME _____

Assessment

Part 1: I understand equivalent fractions.

Write the equivalent fractions.

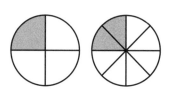 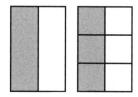 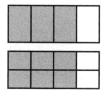

1. _____ = _____   **2.** _____ = _____   **3.** _____ = _____

To find an equivalent fraction, multiply the numerator and denominator by the number in the circle.

4. $\frac{3}{6}$ = ___ ④   **5.** $\frac{2}{3}$ = ___ ⑤   **6.** $\frac{1}{6}$ = ___ ⑥   **7.** $\frac{1}{3}$ = ___ ⑨

Part 2: I can compare fractions.

Write a fraction for the shaded area of each shape. Then, write >, <, or = to compare the fractions.

1.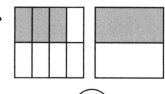

___ ◯ ___

2.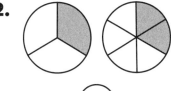

___ ◯ ___

3.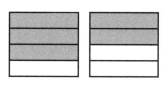

___ ◯ ___

4.

___ ◯ ___

Write >, <, or = to compare the fractions.

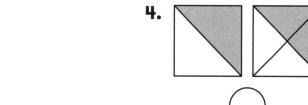

5. $\frac{3}{8}$ ◯ $\frac{10}{12}$ **6.** $\frac{2}{8}$ ◯ $\frac{1}{4}$ **7.** $\frac{1}{5}$ ◯ $\frac{2}{10}$ **8.** $\frac{1}{3}$ ◯ $\frac{2}{4}$

Assessment

Part 3: I can add and subtract fractions and mixed numbers with like denominators.

Add or subtract. Give answers in simplest form.

1.  + = _____

2. 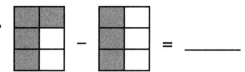 − = _____

3. $\dfrac{1}{4}$
$+\dfrac{1}{4}$
_____

4. $\dfrac{8}{9}$
$-\dfrac{1}{9}$
_____

5. $\dfrac{5}{12}$
$+\dfrac{3}{12}$
_____

6. $\dfrac{5}{10}$
$-\dfrac{3}{10}$
_____

7. $1\dfrac{1}{5}$
$+3\dfrac{3}{5}$
_____

8. $2\dfrac{4}{10}$
$+7\dfrac{4}{10}$
_____

9. $5\dfrac{4}{14}$
$+4\dfrac{5}{14}$
_____

10. $3\dfrac{3}{10}$
$+3\dfrac{2}{10}$
_____

11. $6\dfrac{1}{5}$
$-3\dfrac{3}{5}$
_____

12. $4\dfrac{3}{10}$
$-3\dfrac{7}{10}$
_____

13. $8\dfrac{2}{5}$
$-5\dfrac{4}{5}$
_____

14. $10\dfrac{5}{12}$
$-7\dfrac{7}{12}$
_____

Solve. Give answers in simplest form.

15. A deli customer bought $\frac{10}{16}$ of a pound of ham and $\frac{7}{16}$ of a pound of turkey. How much more ham did she buy than turkey?

_____ of a pound

16. Rain lasted for 3 days. Daily rainfall totals were $\frac{3}{8}$ inch, $3\frac{1}{8}$ inch, and $\frac{5}{8}$ inch. What was the total rainfall?

_____ inches

Assessment

Part 4: I can multiply fractions by whole numbers.

Write each fraction as the product of a whole number and a unit fraction (a fraction with a numerator of 1).

1. _____

2. _____

Multiply. Write answers in simplest form.

3. $6 \times \dfrac{3}{5} =$ _____

4. $2 \times \dfrac{5}{9} =$ _____

5. $\dfrac{2}{7} \times 3 =$ _____

6. $7 \times \dfrac{3}{4} =$ _____

7. $\dfrac{8}{9} \times 4 =$ _____

8. $\dfrac{1}{2} \times 8 =$ _____

9. $\dfrac{4}{5} \times 6 =$ _____

10. $9 \times \dfrac{1}{3} =$ _____

11. $5 \times \dfrac{3}{10} =$ _____

12. $\dfrac{2}{3} \times 3 =$ _____

13. $9 \times \dfrac{7}{8} =$ _____

14. $\dfrac{6}{11} \times 7 =$ _____

Solve. Write answers in simplest form.

15. A class has 20 students. One-fifth of the students are in the hall. How many students are in the hall?

_____ students

16. A hexagon measures $\frac{5}{8}$ inch per side. What is the hexagon's perimeter?

_____ inches

Assessment

Part 5: I understand decimal numbers.

Write a decimal number and a fraction for each model.

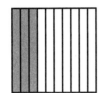 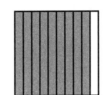 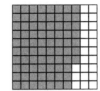

1. _____ or _____   2. _____ or _____   3. _____ or _____

Write each fraction as a decimal.

4. $\frac{3}{10} =$ _____   **5.** $\frac{50}{100} =$ _____   **6.** $\frac{87}{100} =$ _____   **7.** $\frac{9}{100} =$ _____

Solve.

8. $\frac{5}{10} = \frac{}{100}$ **9.** $\frac{80}{100} = \frac{}{10}$ **10.** $\begin{array}{r} \frac{4}{10} \\ + \frac{3}{100} \\ \hline \end{array}$ **11.** $\begin{array}{r} \frac{78}{100} \\ + \frac{2}{10} \\ \hline \end{array}$

Part 6: I can compare decimal numbers to hundredths.

Write >, <, or = to compare the decimal numbers.

1. 0.86 ◯ 0.68   **2.** 0.04 ◯ 0.4   **3.** 0.8 ◯ 0.85

4. 0.5 ◯ 0.6   **5.** 0.99 ◯ 1.0   **6.** 0.77 ◯ 0.82

7. 1.1 ◯ 0.11   **8.** 0.2 ◯ 0.22   **9.** 0.1 ◯ 0.01

Answer Key

Page 8

1. ; **2.** $\frac{4}{8} = \frac{2}{4}$; **3.** $\frac{3}{18}$; **4.** $\frac{3}{4}$; **5.** 6, 6;

6. 5, 5; **7.** $\frac{16}{20}$; **8.** $\frac{1}{3}$

Page 9

1. $\frac{3}{4} = \frac{6}{8}$; **2.** $\frac{2}{2} = 1$; **3.** $\frac{3}{7} = \frac{6}{14}$; **4.** $\frac{1}{5} = \frac{2}{10}$;
5. $\frac{1}{6} = \frac{2}{12}$; **6.** $\frac{8}{8} = 1$; **7.** $\frac{10}{14}$; **8.** $\frac{12}{24}$; **9.** $\frac{8}{32}$; **10.** $\frac{6}{36}$;
11. $\frac{9}{27}$; **12.** $\frac{20}{30}$; **13.** $\frac{10}{25}$; **14.** $\frac{2}{16}$; **15.** $\frac{8}{16}$; **16.** $\frac{2}{3}$;
17. $\frac{5}{8}$; **18.** $\frac{3}{12}$; **19.** $\frac{10}{20}$; **20.** $\frac{15}{25}$; **21.** $\frac{10}{40}$; **22.** $\frac{4}{12}$;
23. Cross out $\frac{2}{6}$. **24.** Cross out $\frac{8}{16}$.

Page 10

1. ; **2.** ; **3.** $\frac{1}{3} < \frac{3}{6}$;

4. $\frac{2}{6} = \frac{4}{12}$; **5.** $\frac{9}{12} > \frac{8}{12}$; **6.** $\frac{12}{24} < \frac{15}{24}$;
7. $\frac{8}{20} > \frac{5}{20}$; **8.** $\frac{5}{10} < \frac{6}{10}$

Page 11

1. $\frac{3}{4} > \frac{2}{4}$; **2.** $\frac{1}{4} = \frac{2}{8}$; **3.** $\frac{3}{8} < \frac{1}{2}$; **4.** $\frac{1}{3} > \frac{2}{8}$; **5.** >;
6. <; **7.** <; **8.** =; **9.** >; **10.** >; **11.** >; **12.** =;
13. <; **14.** <; **15.** =; **16.** =

Page 12

1. Student should shade $\frac{3}{4}$ of shape.
2. Student should shade $\frac{2}{6}$ of shape.
3. $\frac{1}{5} + \frac{2}{5} + \frac{1}{5} = \frac{4}{5}$; **4.** $\frac{6}{8} - \frac{2}{8} - \frac{2}{8} = \frac{2}{8}$; **5.** $\frac{11}{15}$;
6. $\frac{4}{9}$; **7.** $\frac{7}{8}$; **8.** $\frac{6}{14} = \frac{3}{7}$

Page 13

1. Answers will vary. Possible answers:
$\frac{3}{8} + \frac{3}{8} + \frac{1}{8} = \frac{7}{8}$, $\frac{8}{8} - \frac{1}{8} = \frac{7}{8}$; **2.** Answers will vary.
Possible answers: $\frac{10}{16} + \frac{2}{16} + \frac{2}{16} = \frac{14}{16}$, $\frac{15}{16} - \frac{1}{16} = \frac{14}{16}$;

3. Answers will vary. Possible answers:
$\frac{5}{10} + \frac{2}{10} = \frac{7}{10}$, $\frac{8}{10} - \frac{1}{10} = \frac{7}{10}$; **4.** $\frac{3}{4}$; **5.** $\frac{1}{4}$; **6.** $\frac{4}{5}$; **7.** $\frac{1}{4}$;
8. $\frac{3}{5}$; **9.** $\frac{4}{9}$; **10.** $\frac{2}{5}$; **11.** $\frac{4}{5}$; **12.** $\frac{2}{5}$; **13.** $\frac{2}{3}$;
14. 1; **15.** $\frac{9}{10}$; **16.** $\frac{4}{5}$; **17.** $\frac{2}{11}$; **18.** $\frac{7}{9}$; **19.** $\frac{2}{5}$;
20. $\frac{2}{9}$

Page 14

1. $3\frac{2}{3}$; **2.** Student should shade 2 whole
shapes and 2 parts of the third shape. **3.** $3\frac{1}{5}$;
4. $\frac{25}{6}$; **5.** $8\frac{3}{5}$; **6.** $2\frac{2}{9}$; **7.** $\frac{63}{5} + \frac{34}{5} = \frac{97}{5} = 19\frac{2}{5}$;
8. $\frac{101}{12} - \frac{34}{12} = \frac{67}{12} = 5\frac{7}{12}$

Page 15

1. $\frac{6}{5}$ or $1\frac{1}{5}$; **2.** $\frac{7}{3}$ or $2\frac{1}{3}$; **3.** $\frac{11}{4}$ or $2\frac{3}{4}$;
4. $\frac{17}{6}$ or $2\frac{5}{6}$; **5.** $12\frac{1}{5}$; **6.** $9\frac{1}{2}$; **7.** $5\frac{1}{7}$; **8.** $7\frac{7}{11}$;
9. 8; **10.** $12\frac{2}{3}$; **11.** $3\frac{1}{3}$; **12.** $2\frac{3}{5}$; **13.** $2\frac{1}{5}$;
14. $5\frac{1}{11}$; **15.** $1\frac{1}{5}$; **16.** 1

Page 16

1. $\frac{3}{4}$; **2.** $\frac{3}{4}$; **3.** $\frac{6}{3}$; **4.** $\frac{6}{3}$; **5.** $\frac{7}{10}$; **6.** $\frac{15}{19}$; **7.** $\frac{4}{6} = \frac{2}{3}$;
8. $\frac{32}{5} = 6\frac{2}{5}$

Page 17

1. $1\frac{3}{7}$; **2.** $2\frac{2}{5}$; **3.** $5\frac{1}{4}$; **4.** $1\frac{1}{2}$; **5.** $1\frac{1}{7}$; **6.** $\frac{3}{4}$;
7. $2\frac{2}{3}$; **8.** $\frac{3}{5}$; **9.** $2\frac{2}{3}$; **10.** 2; **11.** $1\frac{1}{2}$; **12.** $\frac{3}{4}$;
13. $1\frac{7}{8}$; **14.** $\frac{2}{3}$; **15.** 3; **16.** $3\frac{8}{9}$; **17.** $1\frac{1}{6}$;
18. $2\frac{4}{7}$; **19.** $2\frac{1}{2}$; **20.** 4; **21.** $\frac{4}{5}$; **22.** $3\frac{1}{3}$;
23. $1\frac{5}{7}$; **24.** $1\frac{1}{5}$

Page 18

1. $\frac{1}{8} + \frac{2}{8} + \frac{3}{8} = \frac{6}{8} = \frac{3}{4}$; **2.** $\frac{52}{6} - \frac{17}{6} = \frac{35}{6} = 5\frac{5}{6}$;
3. $\frac{1}{10} \times 5 = \frac{5}{10} = \frac{1}{2}$; **4.** $12 \times \frac{2}{3} = \frac{24}{3} = 8$

Answer Key

Page 19
1. $1\frac{3}{4}$; **2.** $\frac{5}{7}$; **3.** $3\frac{1}{3}$; **4.** $\frac{1}{4}$; **5.** $\frac{5}{6}$; **6.** $1\frac{1}{3}$;
7. $2\frac{1}{12}$; **8.** $2\frac{2}{3}$

Page 20
1.
2.

3. 0.9; **4.** 0.42; **5.** $\frac{60}{100}$; **6.** $\frac{81}{100}$;
7. $\frac{40}{100} + \frac{33}{100} = \frac{73}{100}$; **8.** $\frac{20}{100} + \frac{63}{100} = \frac{83}{100}$

Page 21
1. $\frac{4}{10}$, 0.4; **2.** $\frac{2}{10}$, 0.2; **3.** $\frac{5}{10}$, 0.5; **4.** $\frac{21}{100}$, 0.21;
5. $\frac{47}{100}$, 0.47; **6.** $\frac{34}{100}$, 0.34; **7.** $\frac{1}{100} + \frac{90}{100} = \frac{91}{100}$;
8. $\frac{30}{100} + \frac{7}{100} = \frac{37}{100}$; **9.** $\frac{9}{100} + \frac{90}{100} = \frac{99}{100}$;
10. $\frac{110}{100} + \frac{11}{100} = \frac{121}{100} = 1\frac{21}{100}$;
11. $\frac{2}{100} + \frac{30}{100} = \frac{32}{100} = \frac{8}{25}$; **12.** $\frac{50}{100} + \frac{7}{100} = \frac{57}{100}$

Page 22
1. $\frac{42}{100}$, $\frac{26}{100}$, Circle 0.42 and $\frac{42}{100}$. **2.** 0.6, 0.3,
Circle 0.3. **3.**

4.
Ones	Decimal Point	Tenths	Hundredths
0	.	8	5
0	.	5	8

5. =; **6.** <

Page 23
1.
2.

Page 24
Solve: Proficient students will recognize that both Caleb and Marissa are correct because $\frac{2}{4}$, $\frac{8}{16}$, and $\frac{1}{2}$ are all equivalent fractions. The numerator and denominator of $\frac{2}{4}$ can be divided by 2 to create the equivalent fraction $\frac{1}{2}$ or multiplied by 4 to create the equivalent fraction $\frac{8}{16}$.

Reflect: Answers will vary. Possible answers: If might be useful to divide a 50-cent piece ($\frac{1}{2}$ of a dollar) into 2 quarters ($\frac{2}{4}$ of a dollar). It might be useful to divide a half-pound bag of candy into 8 individual bags that each contain one ounce (or $\frac{1}{16}$ of a pound).

Page 25
Solve: Proficient students will recognize that Virginia has eaten $\frac{4}{6}$ or $\frac{2}{3}$ of the pizza, leaving $\frac{1}{3}$ uneaten. Using visual models or equivalent fractions, students will discover that $\frac{1}{3}$ is greater than $\frac{1}{4}$, so Virginia does have enough pizza left in order to give her brother $\frac{1}{4}$ of the original pizza.

Reflect: To be fair, Virginia should give her brother the remaining slices of pizza ($\frac{2}{6}$ or $\frac{1}{3}$ of the original pizza), since Virginia has already eaten $\frac{2}{3}$ of the pizza herself.

Page 24
3. >; **4.** <; **5.** >; **6.** <; **7.** <; **8.** <; **9.** >;
10. >; **11.** >; **12.** >; **13.** <; **14.** >; **15.** <;
16. <; **17.** <

Answer Key

Page 26

Solve: Proficient students will change the mixed number $2\frac{5}{12}$ to the improper fraction $\frac{29}{12}$ and subtract $\frac{8}{12}$ (which represents an 8-inch section of a foot made up of 12 inches) to find the difference $\frac{21}{12}$, which is equivalent to $1\frac{9}{12}$ or $1\frac{3}{4}$ feet.

Reflect: Students' drawings should show a 3-foot yardstick of which 1 foot, 9 inches is shaded.

Page 27

Solve: Proficient students will multiply the whole number 60 (items of clothing in Hector's closet) by the fraction $\frac{3}{5}$ to find that $\frac{180}{5}$ or 36 items have stripes and by the fraction $\frac{1}{4}$ to find that $\frac{60}{4}$ or 15 items are pants. Since no pants are striped, students can use the equation $60 - 36 - 15 = 9$ to find that 9 is the greatest number of items of clothing that could be shirts without stripes.

Reflect: Answers will vary. Possible answer: A number line divided into 60 equal parts could show that 36 parts represent clothing items with stripes, 15 parts represent clothing items that are pants, and the remaining 9 parts represent items that could be shirts without stripes.

Page 28

Solve: Proficient students will sort the tiles into those closest to 0 (0.09, 0.21, and another tile the student creates such as 0.15), those closest to 0.5 (0.43, 0.67, and another tile the student creates such as 0.55), and those closest to 1 (0.76, 0.9, 1.05).

Reflect: Any number greater than 0.25 would be closer to 0.5 than to 0. So, a tile that belongs with those closest to 0 would have at most 2 tenths.

Assessment

Part 1: 1. $\frac{1}{4} = \frac{2}{8}$; **2.** $\frac{1}{2} = \frac{3}{6}$; **3.** $\frac{3}{4} = \frac{6}{8}$; **4.** $\frac{12}{24}$; **5.** $\frac{10}{15}$; **6.** $\frac{6}{36}$; **7.** $\frac{9}{27}$

Part 2: 1. $\frac{3}{8} < \frac{1}{2}$; **2.** $\frac{1}{3} = \frac{2}{6}$; **3.** $\frac{3}{4} > \frac{2}{4}$; **4.** $\frac{1}{2} = \frac{2}{4}$; **5.** <; **6.** =; **7.** =; **8.** <

Part 3: 1. $\frac{3}{4}$; **2.** $\frac{1}{6}$; **3.** $\frac{1}{2}$; **4.** $\frac{7}{9}$; **5.** $\frac{2}{3}$; **6.** $\frac{1}{5}$; **7.** $4\frac{4}{5}$; **8.** $9\frac{4}{5}$; **9.** $9\frac{9}{14}$; **10.** $6\frac{1}{2}$; **11.** $2\frac{3}{5}$; **12.** $\frac{3}{5}$; **13.** $2\frac{3}{5}$; **14.** $2\frac{5}{6}$; **15.** $\frac{3}{16}$ of a pound; **16.** $4\frac{1}{8}$ inches

Part 4: 1. $3 \times \frac{1}{4} = \frac{3}{4}$; **2.** $5 \times \frac{1}{6} = \frac{5}{6}$; **3.** $3\frac{3}{5}$; **4.** $1\frac{1}{9}$; **5.** $\frac{6}{7}$; **6.** $5\frac{1}{4}$; **7.** $3\frac{5}{9}$; **8.** 4; **9.** $4\frac{4}{5}$; **10.** 3; **11.** $1\frac{1}{2}$; **12.** 2; **13.** $7\frac{7}{8}$; **14.** $3\frac{9}{11}$; **15.** 4 students; **16.** $3\frac{3}{4}$ inches

Part 5: 1. $\frac{3}{10}$, 0.3; **2.** $\frac{9}{10}$, 0.9; **3.** $\frac{77}{100}$, 0.77; **4.** 0.3; **5.** 0.5; **6.** 0.87; **7.** 0.09; **8.** $\frac{50}{100}$; **9.** $\frac{8}{10}$; **10.** $\frac{43}{100}$; **11.** $\frac{98}{100}$

Part 6: 1. >; **2.** <; **3.** <; **4.** <; **5.** <; **6.** <; **7.** >; **8.** <; **9.** >

Notes